T0194001

SPICE UP Your SOUL

SPICE UP Your SOUL

RELATIONSHIP

JENNY CAILING PUGH

iUniverse

SPICE UP YOUR SOUL
RELATIONSHIP

iUniverse books may be ordered through booksellers or by contacting:

iUniverse
1663 Liberty Drive
Bloomington, IN 47403
www.iuniverse.com
1-800-Authors (1-800-288-4677)

ISBN: 978-1-5320-9894-9 (sc)
ISBN: 978-1-5320-9898-7 (e)

Print information available on the last page.

iUniverse rev. date: 04/08/2020

Contents

Part 2: Featured Best Friends of My Whole Life

Introduction

This is the third book in my general title Spice Up your Soul. The first book is in that title alone, the second is Spice Up Your Soul with the subtitle Beautiful Soul Beautiful Life and now I am publishing my third book under the General title Spice Up Your Soul with the subtitle Relationships.

My main objective in writing all these books is to share with people of all ages and all walks of life and in all cultures my experiences in handling any situations in life, may it be a dream to come true and most important to solve problems that we come across as we continue to live the life that God and Nature has intended us to enjoy.

There are so many areas in our lives that we should deal with. Even in our dreams and wishes to change our life situations to something that we surmise to be a better life for us as a person and for our family, if we fail to achieve them will makes us feel so bad that we tend to forget that we have a very powerful soul deep within us who is able and willing to make our dreams come true. My main objective in my writings is not only to remind us of such powerhouse within each of us but most important to help the readers see, familiarize and use such power from within to work in our every day lives hence keeping us alive and enjoy a beautiful and wonderful life that God and Nature has intended for each of us to enjoy.

Relationships with everything and everyone around us is a significant aspect in life that we have to deal with in a very personal level. In this book I discuss about the various types of relationships that we encounter as we journey on in life. This reminds me of an old adage which says "Tell me who your companions are and I will tell you who you are."

The objective of this book is to open our minds to these various relationships to work harmoniously in our lives and to remind the readers that each person is what he/she as a result of what kind and quality of relationships he had been through and whether these relationships cause him to become a better person and to improve the quality of his life and/or do these relationships pull him down to the abyss of hopelessness and despair.

Everything that is happening in our lives is a result of the quality of relationships that we had learned to embrace; are you generally happy in your relationships or otherwise?

Have a comprehensive introspection using the contents of my book Relationship.

Are you Happy?

"Are you happy?" This simple question is often asked by a friend or love ones in various occasions; whether they mean to know exactly the answer or not, the fact remains that the answer could mean a meaningful life if we take it seriously.

Let Me Cite Some Very Good Reasons to be Happy;(I am speaking for myself; see if it works with you too).

1. **I am happiest ever since the moment I had sincerely accepted myself as beautiful and had started to love myself unconditionally.**

I used to see myself as an "ugly duckling" feeling like I was born a mistake. I felt like everything about me was ugly; too wide face, too tiny nose, too big eyes and eye bags, too curly hair, too thick lips, too long and skinny legs; and so forth and so on. It was really a very disturbing feeling which prevented me from pursuing my dreams.

Then one day I had decided to do something about it before I could ever start on whatever pursuit I had. I had decided to attend to myself first wholeheartedly. So I took it religiously to daily affirm in words, spoken and written, myself as being beautiful and to accept and to love myself completely as I am. It worked; I was able to convince myself as beautiful and lovable so that no matter what my sister and friends tease me on my legs and other physical flaws, I still feel beautiful and unique.

Won't you be happy knowing that you are beautiful and lovable? They don't have to agree with you. What is important is; this is how you see yourself in the deepest sense.

Feeling ugly and non-acceptance of your physical flaws is self-defeating and can block you from following your dreams to success; especially when part of your dreams involves social functions and socialization. To feel ugly is such a sad state of mind. Nobody is actually ugly in the true sense.

2. Being creative is another reason to be happy.

Life is a lifetime of moment by moment continuous flow of thoughts. In every second of your life, even when you are sleeping, your mind does not stop thinking and it is thinking millions of thoughts every single moment, whether you are aware of it or not. What is worse is that you are not aware if those thoughts are happy thoughts, memories, analyses, and many other mental processes. What if most of those thoughts that you are not aware of are sad or angry thoughts? Worst still is if those thoughts which you are aware of or having deliberate and dominating negative intentions are the ones that are controlling your mind. No wonder lots of people are bored, angry, and feeling tired of life without even knowing the reasons why.

The most effective remedy to at least alter the thought processes and redirect them consciously to a happy and productive one is to be creative.

To be creative is not only in the arts, it can be physical activities, writing, or any hobbies that make you feel whole or happy about yourself.

3. Being Loved and to Love is a happy state of being

Nothing can compare to the happiness of one who is actually experiencing and enjoying being loved and who can love in the truest sense. Love is a very happy energy that is warming not only the soul but also giving colors to life as a whole. Love begets love; if you love someone unconditionally, you will reap love from him/her/them in multiples. Love is overflowing.

Love is like a seed of any tree or fruit-bearing plants. You plant one seed of love in a very fertile soil and nurture such seed as it grows until it bears fruit; the fruit of such one good seed will yield you thousands even millions of good fruit in its lifetime.

Who do we love? The Bible tells us to love even "your enemies". Well this is tough if we take it literally; we cannot force ourselves to love the "unlovable" and the "misfits" more so the "hateful" enemies. But Love does not qualify, does not "pre-condition" the object of love; and love is freely given without asking for payback. This is the only type of Love that makes us a happy person and which therefore make us enjoy a happy and blessed life in our lifetime.

There are three types if not stages of love. First, we must be a recipient of God's unconditional Love, the **Agape Love.** To be a recipient of such love is to acknowledge the Existence of God or Nature, praise the Greatness of God or Nature, be awed by the Beauty of Nature or God's Creation. We should take time to be in the "presence" of God or Nature; to be connected and establish a certain degree of strong connection; each of us is also part of nature so we should experience "oneness" to the whole Creation or God, or the Universe; whichever suits your conviction. Only then can we experience this Agape Love; the Unconditional Love that once found a seat within us will have its "throne" to Divinely Guide us as we live our lives. This Divine Guidance functions in every aspect of our lives...it Guides, Protects, Provides, and the list continues.

The second type or stage of love is the **Philos**; this is

the kind of love we accord our relationships with any other human beings in our horizon and the whole population in the world. With this kind of love reigning in our hearts, we can allow everybody to be "them"; we won't "attack" or destroy any one's life in any way, rather we offer encouragement freely when needed. We can only have this kind of love if we experience the Agape Love. People can "fake" Philos love according to their selfish and ulterior motives but the truth will come out sooner than they will realize and it will be shown in the troubled life that they will experience. Learning and surrender to the Source of all Love, the Agape, will then be the only solution. Philos love will be noticeable by people surrounding us, if we have this; we will be popular and be known as an "authentic", reliable, trustworthy, understanding, among others.

In this kind of love also falls the love for parents, children, relatives, associates, best friends, etc.

The third kind or stage of Love is the **Eros Love**; it is so called because of its natural tendency to be erotic or erroneous, well not literally erotic in the normal sense. This is the love we accord our husband or wife. This is the most sensual and emotional love and can easily be diverted into mere sexual pleasure and lust. This is the most destructive love if not supported by high moral values; hence instead of this love to be a blessing it becomes a curse to humanity and yet people won't realize it. This is the kind of love that blindfolds humanity so that everybody goes down to the pit of destruction. This Eros Love could only be a blessing, a gift of joy and happiness, and be successful if we have **Agape Love** and **Philos Love** in the background; other than being backed-up or founded in the Agape and Philos Love, Eros is a tool to destroy humanity in every turn. Just observe what is going on with this kind of relationships these days. Divorce, broken homes, scandals in high places, juvenile criminals as a result of broken homes...look at statistics; the list is endless destruction of human values and lives. And nature is angered resulting to natural disasters and calamities. Can you connect? No, you won't even believe it; but believe it or not. The Bible says "Let those who have eyes see, and those who have ears hear..." Humanity is carnal and spiritually blind; it needs a Love higher than what they are only familiar of.

The Universe Has Provided All the Reasons to be Happy

I had discussed only three basic reasons to be happy in this life but sure I can do much better, given the time and space. This world contains all the reasons to be happy if we see it that way and if we know the Universal Laws the govern it; and most important, knowing is just basic, we should learn to Live What We Know, otherwise head knowledge will just confuse us. The trick is: Live and Experience all you Learn and Know...don't just talk about it.

1

A PERSPECTIVE IN RELATIONSHIPS

Everything in this universe is interrelated whether we agree or not. Every person is related to every human to every plant, to every animal, to everything created by human or everything natural in the whole ecosystem. There is a parallel relationship of your life to everything in the whole ecosystem. The quality of your life depends so much on the quality of your relationship to everything around you. Previously I had discussed all types of relationship that are known but it doesn't mean that they are the only types of relationships there is. There are still many unknown things in this universe that may never be known by humans and even then, we are still related to the unknown.

Basic to all types of relationship is harmony. If you are in harmony with everything related to you then life is wonderful beyond you can imagine. To establish a harmonious relationship with everything in your life is first of all to develop and maintain a harmonious relationship with yourself within you. Maintain a happy disposition and be thankful for everything that you are and you have. Avoid complaining about anything, instead introspect and meditate on what is good in you and your life and in everyone and everything around you.

Happiness lingers on in a life that is in harmony with everything in the whole ecosystem. Nature grants you the desires of your heart when you are in harmony in all your relationships. Harmony starts with forgiving, forgiving yourself, your loved ones even your enemies; forgiving is a power that draws miracles to your life and keeps you in harmony with every relationship you come across.

2

RELATIONSHIPS

Humans are social beings. No man is an island as the saying goes. Even in the Bible at creation God added another human being, Eve, to Adam because God knows how lonely Adam would have been by living alone.

Life would be lonely, sad, miserable, deprived, poor and devoid of any excitement and enthusiasm without any relationship at all.

But relationship is not just with another human; we have some types of relationships as follow;

1. Relationship with oneself;
2. Relationship with other humans;
3. Relationship with other living things such as plants and animals;
4. Relationship with objects, animate or inanimate.
5. Relationship with God, Nature and the Universe.

Relationships are meant to be beautiful, productive, harmonious and blissful which objective is to keep a person happy and enjoy life. Happy emotions and nourishment are a necessary component to maintain a harmonious relationship.

Relationships should be harmonious otherwise it will lose the essence of its objective. When the relationship sours then separation occurs or else both parties will just hurt each other and destroy each other's' existence eventually.

Next topic will be the discussion on each type of relationship.

3

RELATIONSHIP WITH YOURSELF

In my discussion with the various types of relationship I emphasized five most important types of relationship that can make our lives meaningful and living harmoniously in life.

Life is beautiful only and only if we live harmoniously with everything that we are related to.

Basic to all relationships is the relationship with the self. Following are the basic qualities that one should have with the self;

1. Love yourself unconditionally;
2. Forgive yourself;
3. Accept and embrace all your personal qualities, experiences, situations and conditions in life;
4. You must be all for yourself when everything else point their fingers at you;
5. Be honest with yourself
6. Constantly appreciate yourself for all the good things in you and the good deeds you have done to yourself and others;

7. **Agree and affirm to yourself your innermost desires.**

Remember that if you have a harmonious relationship with yourself, all the rest of your other relationships will be as harmonious and life will be beautiful and abundant for you.

Now I would like to elaborate each of the qualities of relationships I have enumerated above.

Love yourself unconditionally:

Loving yourself unconditionally means loving without pre-qualifying. It's not "loving because..." such as loving because you are the most beautiful or you are the best person you know. It's not comparing yourself to others or it's not a conceited type of loving. It's loving yourself for being alive, creative and having all the potentials of being human. Your attitude of loving yourself unconditionally will overflow so that you can love others too just as well. If you truly love yourself others will follow, they will find you lovable and will love you just as much as you love yourself, do you feel that you are truly lovable?

It's easy to say "I love myself completely as I am" but the question is how do you show your love to yourself, and do you honestly love yourself?

Following are some of the techniques to show yourself that you love him/her.

1. When you get up from sleep in the morning even before you wash your face or comb your hair look

in the mirror and say to your image in the mirror "I love you, you are so beautiful," then smile and continue to say "Oh I love that smile, keep smiling beautiful lady."

2. Write in a piece of bond paper or in your notebook "I am beautiful, I accept and love myself completely as I am." Repeat writing this 100 times in a day and do this for 20 days.

Forgive yourself:

We make mistakes, all humans do, we are not perfect just as the rest of humanity. You see your defects and weaknesses, you have to, you have to admit your mistakes otherwise how and what will you forgive yourself if you don't see what mistakes you do?

Everybody has physical defects too, even beauty queens in the universal levels have physical flaws. You know and see your defects, emotionally, intellectually and physically, you have to know and see them in yourself yet even with all these defects and flaws you can love yourself unconditionally and you have to forgive yourself for despising yourself for having the defects and flaws. It's only in forgiving yourself that you can love and accept yourself completely and unconditionally.

Sometimes we feel guilty for the wrong doings we accord other people or even to ourselves then we say "I am stupid." That's a big no-no to say to yourself.. Do not make justifications just accept that you did something horribly wrong then forgive yourself and assure yourself that you are capable of not repeating those wrong doings or to do better in a given situation.

Accept and embrace all your personal qualities, experiences, situations and conditions in life:

To accept and embrace your personal qualities, experiences, situations and conditions in life means that there is no place for complaints in your mind and in your whole mental attitudes and behaviors. Do you like the company of a person who complains about just anything around him?

Maintain a grateful attitude and count your blessings. Remember that life is a variety of objects, series of incidents and conditions; if you feel like you are unlucky in life or that none of your wishes and prayers are answered favorably then complaining just perpetuate the condition, complaining doesn't help. To be grateful for what you already possess and experienced helps to invite and multiply your blessings.

If you feel like you are not lucky enough to qualify as beautiful physically or as intelligent as you wish you should be, then don't be sad or angry with yourself or your parents or God, such attitude won't help to change the situation; think of something that could make you feel better and thank God you are alive equipped with a creative mind that is capable of making some changes and start counting your blessings.

You must be all for yourself when everything else point their fingers at you

Nobody and nothing can let you down if you won't allow it. Remember to take your side in any conflict because nobody else knows you as much as you know yourself. No one else is with you every second of your life throughout your life so be a reliable and dependable person for yourself.

Constantly appreciate yourself for all the good things in you and the good deeds you have done to yourself and others.

Write down or talk to yourself quietly or aloud enumerating those happy moments and your true self.

Self-talk yourself like the following;

1. I am beautiful.
2. I am intelligent.
3. I am creative.
4. I am rich.
5. I am healthy.
6. I am lovable.

And more similar to all these whether you can believe it or not just self-talk yourself repeatedly with those wonderful words that you can imagine for yourself.

Agree and affirm to yourself your innermost desires.

Honor your desires and dream or imagine yourself already having those dreams come true. See yourself living in the dream. This is one way of agreeing with yourself and honoring your desires.

4

RELATIONSHIP WITH GOD

Ever since time immemorial, history accounts for human beings' relationship with God or any other Spiritual beings.

The fact the we are souls only implies that we are not only physical but most importantly we are also spiritual beings in the physical embodiment. Our thoughts and emotions largely determine, direct and control our life situation and condition in the material plane of life. What you think, dream, desire and wish and plan for your life to become and happen are the works of the spirit world. You cannot see thoughts, dreams, desires and wishes of any human being unless he expresses them in words or draw or sketch and illustrate them in writing and in any devices to show its form and actual appearance.

Since these intangible inner works of our minds and soul are not seen, everyone is free to create his hidden world according to his desire and purpose. What is within so is the without of any human being. This means that what you create, imagine and dream of manifest in your material life.

But it is sad to observe that many people would say that they are just good in dreaming and imagining about beautiful things in life that could happen to them but none of these happen in their real life or material life. Do you agree with this notion? What happens to the saying "What you think is what you are or what you become?"

The difference lies in the fact that most people have not truly established rapport or tight relationship with the Almighty God or the Higher Spiritual Being who can make everything possible for the life of those humans who ask, believe, and claim what is intended for them in the individual level.

In every relationship to become harmonious and productive, communication is the prerequisite. Do you feel personal relationship with your God? Notice that I say "your God". This means that your God may be Allah, Jesus, or any Spiritual Being that you have strong connection in the personal level. Personal relationship with the Spiritual Being means that you have lived all your life being guided by this Being in every step you take in your life's journey.

None of us mortal beings have the right to judge anyone who does not believe in the God that we believe to be the only true God. If your God is true for you, others may have a God who is also true for them. The truth is every person in this planet is a true creature of God and a true part of this Universe and whoever these people believe to be the true God based on his personal experience is also true.

What is most important is the quality of relationship one has established with the God who he believes to be the true God. It is not necessary to belong to a certain religious sect in order to establish a stable relationship with God or the powerful Spiritual Being in your life.

Having this very strong relationship with God is in itself a blessing in any relationship a person can have in the material plane. Harmonious relationship with the God of your life is equivalent to harmonious relationship a person can have with anyone and anything else in this life.

A real and functional personal relationship with God happens in the individual level. It's not religious affiliation that can establish a strong relationship with God. Religion is a cultural thing which means a person believes in a god that his social group believes. Be that it may no one can judge what a group or a person believes to be the true God, their god might have done wonders in their collective or personal lives and you might think it is foolish to believe in what others believe. God can only be real in the life of a person who in his journey through this life he experiences the spiritual presence in every step of his journey.

Let me discuss a little on what kind of experience a person could have with his god. A person who have a real relationship and experience with his god knows his presence particularly in his time of needs. It is a normal thing for a god-believer hopeless human to ask God to help him in his time of dire need and when his needs are solved or supplied after asking God in the form of prayers then he will begin to and continue to call God or pray even if he is not in need just to thank and Praise His God for any gifts and blessings he receives at any point of his life.

5

RELATIONSHIP WITH NATURE

Relationship with God is the highest form of relationship, it is highest in the sense that it encompasses human type of relationship. When your relationship with God or the Highest Spiritual Being that you have learned to develop your faith into through your personal experience is strongly established you will notice that your any other types of relationship become harmonious. That is how powerful the relationship with God is in your life. There is nothing anymore in your life that can cause you fear. All imaginary fears such as fear of poverty, fear for evil things to come to you will banish. You will live in faith, trust, hope and love in your daily life by the moment.

Your world become beautiful and you can see the beauty of nature. Everything in nature is there for us to learn to develop a beautiful life for ourselves in the personal level.

When you behold the vast ocean, your mind will automatically contemplate on abundance in your life; the ocean never dries and your mind makes a parallel with your life it will remind you that you will have abundance of everything in your life. Likewise, with the sands in the beach, the leaves of the trees, the stars up in the heavenly space, they are not only in incomparable exquisiteness to lift up your spirit but also to remind us on how God supplies all our needs according to the beauty and infinity of all the beautiful things in nature.

To establish a close relationship with nature is to constantly spend some time with it and try to understand the meaning of its beauty that it is conveying to you. When you feel sad and lonely go out to the meadow, watch the beautiful wild flowers with various shapes and colors that are swayed by the gentle breeze, hear the singing birds that nature freely entertain you, understand the meaning, the melody of joy to cheer you. When you think you are poor go to the wood and try to count all the leaves of the trees or start star-gazing at the stars on a starry night, count as many as you can and know that as countless as the stars in the sky and the sands in the beach so are the ways that Nature provides for you.

If you love nature and has developed a durable relationship with it, you will see the parallel in your life that nature is conveying to you, you will understand the beauty and purpose of your life, you will understand what it is telling you according to beauty, creativity and abundance, your wisdom will guide you in all your endeavors and you will be blessed throughout your life.

6

RELATIONSHIPS WITH NATURAL OR IMAGINARY BEINGS

My last topic was relationship with nature. Now it's relationship with natural or imaginary beings.

It has been said that no matter how the great minds conduct studies about what is there to be known and discovered in this planet and the whole universe, humans are allowed only 10% of what really exist in this world. The unknown and that could never be known by humans are far greater than what is already known. It's 90% unknown as opposed to just 10% known. This 10% knowledge of the truth that exist in this world is in fact very spectacular and a great wonder to humanity. Curing cancer is one example of the unknown.

The fact that humans are incapable of knowing everything in this world only reinforces the logical idea of maintaining faith and trust to the God or spiritual beings that coexist with us in this world.

Belief or faith to the unknown is a valid assumption just as negatives are valid elements even in Mathematics. The unknown is a reality. People often believe on something they can touch, see or hear but just because they cannot see, hear or touch something does not mean they don't exist.

Take for example a situation where a born blind man never see light, it does not mean that just because he cannot see light that light does not exist. For him who is blind the literal light does not exist, that's true but for everyone else who has normal and functional eyesight, light is a reality.

We can derive a parallel to this assumption take the situation of a person who would say that he has seen an angel and he truly believes in angels but the person who had never experienced seeing an angel, which in this case is most people don't see angels, does not mean that angels don't exist just because they don't see one in their whole life.

Many people strive to learn to possess supernatural powers or abilities so that they too can experience some miracles in their lives. Many would do rituals, spells and other sorts of magical practices in order to achieve their goals. The fact is, this ability to possess supernatural powers is a gift, freely granted to the person who has knowingly or unknowingly stumbled into the realm of higher spirituality.

The only thing we can do is to establish strong faith and stable relationship in certain spiritual beings that you had learned to believe through your experience.

One question remains, what type of spiritual beings have you learned to believe? Check yourself, angels are good spiritual beings as opposed to monsters or vampires and the like. To establish relationship with wholesome spiritual beings will bring you lots of blessings and miracles as opposed to believing in scary beings, such belief can cause disasters such as accidents, incurable disease and the likes into your life.

To believe in the existence of these spiritual beings is a personal matter, no one has the right to judge others when it comes to one's experience and relationship with spiritual beings. Many people choose to disbelieve in any of these beings for whatever reason. Their minds are not open to the fact that just because they don't see, hear, touch these beings does not mean that they don't exist.

Those who believe, established a stable relationship with any spiritual beings can prove that their lives are easier and happier because they know a reality that works for them and that most people don't. Their lives are full of miracles in perfect timing, they live a miraculous life. Nothing is lost in believing but you have everything to gain.

By nature human beings are limited to the five senses, some have six senses but that sixth sense is a gift to special few, they are the genius, the psychics and the likes, Would you we say that the Creator of human beings is unfair? my question then "would you say that the Creator is unfair about why some people are black and others are brown or whatever human differences there are?" Nature hates duplication, Nature is diversity and there is beauty in a harmonious diversity where colors, shapes and sizes blend together to create a whole.

By the way, every human being has sixth sense, this sixth only differ in human being in the frequency and usage of its power and ability. Some sixth sense are well developed through constant practice, some few just happen to stumble on the positive and powerful use of his sixth sense while the majority are in the dark, meaning they have no idea what it is hence cannot believe and avail on its power in their lives.

Those whose sixth sense are working in their lives are happy and peaceful humans, they know that there is nothing in life that can let them down because they see (sense) the beginning and end of their existence.

7

RELATIONSHIP WITH OTHER HUMANS

We humans are social beings and as such the quality of our lives in terms of enjoyment depends on how we present ourselves to the world. Our successes in life career wise, financially and social status depend on how people in general see us or perceive our personality. An attractive personality gets lucky in finding the job that he really wants and, in the notion, that an attractive woman finds her perfect mate or the man she dreams to have a lasting relationship with.

In this topic we dwell on the attractive personality. What comprise an attractive personality? Before we answer that question let's define personality as the totality of a person's outward appearance such as beauty or physical attractiveness, health, demeanor or the ways he/she carries himself/herself in front of people, behavior, self-expression in body language and in words and in the way he/she speaks that are influenced by culture, added to that are the natural inclinations, motivations, desires, dreams, philosophy, talents, belief and value system and intelligence.

The inner quality of a person is expressed outwardly through behavior, manner of dressing, speaking prowess and demeanor. An attractive personality does not try hard to be liked by anyone because he is already attractive, lovable or likeable whether he does something or not. You don't need to try to be nice to others if you don't feel and believe that you are truly nice. The best personality is one who is true to himself first of all because being true and honest to one's self is the most attractive personality. Do not try to be someone or something else other than the real you because sooner or later your truth will come out and people will dislike you once they find out that you are just acting.

To have a harmonious relationship with other people, even with those you had never met before have great advantage to you as a person and to your life as a whole. You can only have harmonious relationship with every human including the so-called unlovable if you love yourself unconditionally because this kind of love overflows, you are lovable yourself for others because they perceive your being a loving person.

These days many people who are searching for their other half or life partner have easier means to find one because of the rampant global use of the social media. It is easy to find friends but it is also easier to be fooled because one will not have a perfect way to know the person on the other side. This is the very reason why I suggest that one has to consult his own soul and express to it what you exactly want from the person you are going to have a lasting relationship. Like I say repeatedly, the soul knows what you exactly want and need and it knows the ways and methods to make your wishes and dreams come to material reality. Remember that relationship is under the heading Spice up your soul so the soul must be given importance in everything that we dream, we do and we manifest.

8

FAMILY RELATIONSHIP

When love prevails in the family especially between parents, siblings will also love one another unconditionally. Most often, it is normal that the eldest takes more attention and affection from the parents. Whether intentionally or otherwise, it is a fact that the first born is the first love of the parents, given the marriage is normal; and because of this many siblings that follow after the first-born harbor a secret envy especially when the eldest is an achiever, more beautiful and is always praised by the parents. Sibling rivalry is destructive in the long run; it affects the values formation and self-esteem of the siblings. The eldest may become conceited and may consider his younger siblings as underdogs in the family set up while the younger siblings on the other hand may develop low self-esteem and in everything they do; the motivation is of revenge being challenged to show off what they truly believe to be their personal worth.

It is therefore the responsibility of each member of the

family to maintain harmony in their relationship in any way they can.

Love, respect, and consideration for each member's personality differences are basic requirements to maintain harmonious relationship in the family circle.

A family that is able to maintain peace and harmonious relationship despite individual differences among members will harvest blessings and each will be successful in any fields of specialization that each member endeavors to achieve.

Each sibling should devote to the harmony of the family relationship rather than behaving like you are a burden to the family.

Many broken families are a result to having just one member, say the father or the mother or the eldest child, to carry all the burdens in the family in all aspects especially in the financial supports for the whole family.

Each member of the family has a role to play. The parents work hard to support the children in all their financial needs and this is one of the many important reasons why children should love and respect their parents. The children should do their part in taking care of themselves as well especially in their studies. The children are the parent's dream for a wonderful future, and a wonderful life for the whole family, they are the blessings for the parents and the children should acknowledge their parent's love and dreams for them.

People in a any society love to be closely related to a happy, harmonious and beautiful family hence the social standing of such a family is a blessing by itself.

9

RELATIONSHIP WITH OTHER BLOOD RELATIVES

A side from parents and siblings we have other blood relatives such as grandparents, grandchildren, uncles and aunties, cousins and some distant relatives. To live a life full of blessings we have to have harmonious relationships with other family relatives. They may not be direct family members but they have roles to play in our in our lives that may affect us indirectly.

The idea of maintaining harmonious relationships with everybody and everything we come in contact with must not be taken for granted if you wish to live happily in this life. Living happily means that you are in harmonious relationship with yourself, with parents and siblings, with other blood relatives, with peers, with associates and with everyone you come in contact with.

Like I said, we are all social beings, and everyone we had associated in the process of socialization had contributed in one way or another to our development in the personal level. Even those acquaintances and friends we meet in the social media contribute to or influence our feelings and mental flows. Words are powerful to either inspire or discourage us in any of our endeavors and where do all these words come from? Words are spoken by people whether you know them personally or not and words are more powerful to influence our way of thinking especially when they come from our family members and close relatives.

Let me ask you, who is your close relative in your childhood aside from siblings and parents that you can never forget because you had spent lots of happy moments together? Remember the happy days and the sweet memories with relatives because those moments define the background of your emotional state.

In facebook I met so many relatives that I don't really know in person, we are just relatives because we have the same family name and as we talked, we learned that we are all coming from the same place of origin and this fact convince us all that we are truly blood relatives. I am personally happy to hear from them especially that I grew up knowing only a brother and a sister of my father as blood relatives. My father's brother had 3 kids while his sister had only one child. But I heard many stories from my uncle and my Dad about their childhood experiences with their cousins who we never had met in person. My Dad and his lived in a province away from the city where I grow up with my siblings and parents. Why our Dad never had brought us on vacation to his relatives was a mystery to us, but I know that he would sometimes go on a week vacation to his provincial ancestry.

I have a very special cousin who I love so dearly. She was a great influence in molding my character traits when we were in elementary. She was brilliant in the academe such that she would always end the school year at the top of her class. She was also a champion athlete and was honored in school for that; she represented our school in the district interschools athletic game and she was very popular. She had everything to be proud of herself; she was very pretty, very strong and energetic and most of all she was smart. I may not have all her qualities but I never envied her I was so proud to be the cousin of the most popular pretty and smart champion athlete in our school. But when we grew up to be adults, she was unhappy, she never married and she died of breast cancer at age 60; to say I was sad and grieving is an understatement. What a waste of life.

We love our relatives whether they are achievers or not. In facebook I met some relatives who would message me once in a while Many of them would ask donations for whatever reasons they can formulate. I am happy to give but I have set of rules when it comes to giving If an unknown relative asks financial donations from me, I don't give; I only give to my authentic relative who I know very well in person. It's a principle which says "No one can put you down if you won't allow it," and my father's words which says" "Be humble as a dove but be wise as a serpent" has been my principle as far as giving financial donations to relatives are concerned.

10

SEARCHING FOR A ROMANTIC RELATIONSHIP

There is a season for everything under the sun. There is a time to be just newborn babies then toddlers then kids then teens then adults. The ages from teens to adults are the crucial time for a longing soul to wander and wonder if he can find someone to pay her some special attention and finally love her completely. Human beings dream endlessly and most often they of those things, objects or incidents that they had seen and experienced in their culture, they unknowingly follow what society and culture do. Once a person finds a true love or a romantic relationship, she/he starts to dream of what their life together will bring in the future. Most married couples want to have a family of their own with children to complete their happiness.

But life is not a black and white canvass. Some if not many marriages break for millions of reasons and when that happens a person would again search for a new mate, it's the nature of being human, we never stop until we succeed. This is the purpose of this chapter; how to find your perfect mate. Go on.

Below is an excerpt of the article I wrote and published in hubpages long time ago when I felt romantic love for my husband, I want to share with the readers the language of a romantic heart; we were apart from each other at the time;

It Takes a Lot of Love

One of my favorite hymns when I was young and a Bible woman has these lyrics;

It takes a lot of love to make the world go round;
It takes a lot of kindness too;
It takes a lot of love to calm an angry sound;
To help wounded hearts to heal.

Lord give me love, give me kindness too.
Grant me Thy wisdom Thy will to do;
Help me to live by the golden rules.
Lord give me love.

Love is expressed in many ways. Love is very often the inspiration of songs and poems, short stories and novels. The drama in life revolves around love, regardless of what kind of love it is and whatever the end will be.

Love is a beautiful feeling so enjoy it while it lasts. Some love are faked; well, it's actually not love at all.

The following is another narrative that expresses the emotions of love in a certain time of my existence. In creating this I have someone special in my mind, and this is dedicated to him.

It Takes a Lot of Love...; Secured in Your Love

You are the focus of my life;
My vision of you is a candle in a windless night;
To my left is emptiness; to my right is but darkness;
Backward and upward are non-existing;
For my sight is steady and fixated to your direction.
The chasm between us is unreal; For I am connected to
you in all my affairs;
My thoughts and actions are your "domination";
Everything I do,
I see,
I touch,
I hear,
I smell;
Lead to where you are.
I only live as your embodiment;
In thoughts, in words, in deeds.
Your virility mesmerizes me;
Your charm haunts me;
Your voice is an enchanting melody to my heart;
You are the essence that fuel my day.

You are the trunk;
I am your vine;
You are the kingdom;
I am your domain;
You are the force;
I am the vessel.

You are my reality;
To live for you and with you is my eternity;

Everything else reduces to nothing;
For you and I are entwined;
For you and I are secured;
In the world of bliss that's meant just for you and me.

It's February, the globally traditional month for the romantic hearts. Romantic relationships are the most exciting relationship that a person experiences in his/her whole life. Romantic relationships have several stages as we journey on in life. There are those so-called puppy love, first love, love at first sight, true love, love of my life, eternal love or forever love and the serious love affair that leads to marriage.

In each of these types or stages that happen in a person's life there are processes and stages on how things happen in a given time and how one goes throughout the affairs. If the romantic love is a success in a given time which means you get what you wished for a romantic love, may it be marriage or just a step to learn more in your love life then you must have ventured into the universal realm of a true love. The question then is what kind of relationship are you searching for? Are you into a committed relationship or is it just to experience romance as a passing thing in your life?

The following is what I did when I was searching for a lasting love affair in my "last trip" or last chance for romance.

The Collage That Materialized My Wish for a Romantic relationship

Every now and then everybody wishes for something; these wishes could be objects, people or relationships, and important incidents that seem impossible in a certain time. When these wishes become dominating thoughts that develop into desire, the mind takes over; it starts to surmise on the wistful thinking and the question; "what if I could...?" which triggers the mind to see some possibilities through imagination, observation on his environment and the media; then the mind plans based on its observations and perceptions.

My mind did just that; In September, 2010 while I was living alone in my apartment and teaching at the same time, I suddenly felt lonely which made me say to myself "I wish I had a new husband to love me and care for me and vice versa..." This was also in the second death anniversary of my fiancée. It was just a wish but as the days gone by, such wish was nagging me like it had a life of its own. Then one day while I was sorting out the projects of my students in my bedroom, I noticed the bright red, wide board; it looked so attractive like it was urging me to do something about it and display it somewhere so I picked it and stare at it like something within me was asking what I can do to it.

I sat down, took a pair of scissors and started cutting it with the resulting big heart shape. Without much thinking, I took my big picture from my file and pasted it in the center of the heart. While observing it, I noticed that something was missing so I sorted back my files of pictures and magazines when I saw the picture of Richard Gere that matched the size of my picture so I cut it and pasted it beside my picture and labelled it Richard Gere as opposed to my Jenny under my picture.

I decorated the poster some more and posted it on the wall inside my bedroom; it was placed right beside my dressing table so that I noticed it every morning when I get ready to work. I liked the poster and it made me smile and murmur some crazy loving words to myself every time I happened to glance at it.

When the clock struck 12:00 midnight on February 14, 2011, Greg just arrived in the airport at NAIA, Manila, Philippines, and we had our first hugs.

In retrospect, I noticed that the red heart symbolizes Valentine's Day for me; and some coincidences such as, the fiancée that I was really waiting to come in April, 2011 was named Rick but Greg, who was not my fiancée came on the day of the heart...Greg is double "g", Gere is double "e" such coincidences in the names, heat, and in fact a lot more that I had not mentioned here. Coincidences or is my psyche responsible to this? I am now creating collages that could trigger coincidences for the things I wish for. Such coincidence!

11

HUSBAND AND WIFE RELATIONSHIP

A family starts with a husband and wife relationship but before they become husband and wife, they had to undergo some processes of searching for the right person to be the life partner of the other then the courtship started followed by a romantic relationship. Romantic relationships per se is plagued with intense emotions that fluctuate from love to hatred to jealousy and insecurity and much more in-between.

The most difficult time to start a family is in finding the perfect mate for marriage and this is the very reason why once the man and the woman had decided to marry, they should remain faithful to each other so that they can build a harmonious and prosperous family for themselves and their children in the future.

It has to be remembered that to live a happy and prosperous life one has to understand and live his life in harmonious relationships with himself, other people, his environment and with all objects he come in contact with.

Many miserable lives are caused by broken hearts, broken relationships and entanglements with anything that the person come in contact with in life. If a person does not truly know himself, does not know what he really wants then that is a very good reason that his life would become miserable along the way.

Many men and women had been into a marriage that did not last; Below is my article concerning these marriages;

For the Wives

In the first place you should know why you had chosen the man to be your husband out of the many who had pursued you. Okay, let's see;

You had chosen him because first, you love him.

And why him?

Because he portrays the man of your dreams, the man who made your heart beat faster, the man you can entrust your feelings, your body, and your dreams with. He deserves your love; he deserves to be your partner for life, at least you thought; you can foresee a happy and fulfilling future with him.

In fact it was fine with you not to get married but when this man came along you cannot just ignore and brush off the idea that he met all your requirements for the kind of husband you desired and dreamed off. Wow! What a perfect life!

The twist

Now he is your husband. Happy, to start with, until you discovered his nature. A weakling! No backbones! Disgusting!

Why? He is a <u>liar</u>! ~~Sneaky~~! <u>Cheater</u>!

What did he do?

First, he prepares the way to cheat you.

For <u>distant relationships</u> where the husband is far away in which you just meet regularly in the net; this cheating husband blocks you from all his activities in the net. He <u>hacks</u> you if needed just so you cannot function normally in the internet. He can have <u>access to</u> all your internet activities just so he knows if you might accidentally slip into his secrets; but you won't have access to his. He dates anyone in dating sites and meets them in real for "sex" purposes, eventually. He <u>flirts</u> unlimited; he has all the time to do that because his wife far away is "on schedule" for their chat and has no way of proving her <u>suspicions</u>.

He uses many id's and accounts to camouflage himself and he has fun doing it. He feels very confident that he will never be found by his wife; the idiot doesn't realize that he makes mistakes sometimes; that he forgets sometimes; that he mistakenly sends the <u>flirty message</u> to his wife instead of to his women.

Confrontations

When you confront him, he gets angry and accuses you of accusing him; worse he accuses you of doing what he actually is doing; this is a behavior of a cheater, a liar.

He tries hard to prove that he is decent and having integrity. You don't prove your integrity, people will see, hear, observe and know whether you are trustworthy or having integrity through your values system in words and actions.

The Sad Fact

The sad fact reveals itself. You married a cheater; a weakling; a man with no backbones; a man who is a slave to his basic animal instincts; a man whose pants and genitals are bigger than his head and life as a whole; a man whose happiness is below the belt; a man whose inherent animal instincts are for the sex organs of the opposite sex. A man who needs a decent sex partner for a wife yet cannot control his cravings for promiscuous and loose moral women. A man who hides his weaknesses in the shadow and strength of a decent woman while he continues in his obsessions with the women of his weakling caliber. A man who cannot be contented with just one woman in his life; a man whose prime survival is lascivious sex, and more disgusting and shameful kinky activities and obsessions.

What's worse is he blames his decent wife for his actions; this is very typical for a weakling; he is incapable of accepting his own truth; incapable of seeing what darkness and rotten things he keeps within him. He tries to portray a decent personality of himself and you bought it in the onset, only to discover the shocking truth later.

He is a major <u>disappointment</u> to you.

Always a cheater

First you suspect, it will just be a matter of time when the truth finally reveals itself. Don't try to pry, it will just be a waste of time and energy. It's already good that you are aware of his personality; be <u>vigilant</u> and assertive of the clues. This would be very hard because you will have a lot of arguments between yourselves; but it will pay off one day. If you are wrong in your suspicions and you stick together then be happy. If you find yourself to be wrong and the marriage broke up without you having the chance to prove anything because there was actually nothing to prove, then sit down and check yourself; be happy still because your marriage relationship had actually opened your secret fears for you; and you will do better next time. It's actually a win-win situation.

On the other hand, if you discovered that your suspicions about his cheating had been proven to be true, then congratulate yourself; you had just proven that you can protect yourself from this types of men; this will be one of the basis for your decision-making concerning whether to marry again or to stay single, or on what type of men you will marry in the case where you decide to marry again.

Next is, if you had proven that your husband actually cheated on you, then for God's sake! Let him go immediately! He does not deserve you. Don't give him a second chance to hurt your feelings more than you already are experiencing.

Remember: A CHEATER IS A BORN CHEATER, no excuses.

Don't punish yourself with the weakness of others. It's not your fault that your husband is a weakling. You made a mistake, alright, by wrongfully believing in him in the first place, and worse, loving him...Forgive yourself and let go of him because he cannot help hurting you; it's second nature to him to hurt decent women like you; his type works only for promiscuous and loose moral women and these types of women are everywhere; he will not run short of them and will have more than enough supply of them to go through in his entire life...he just cannot stop being him.

Get rid of him instantly before you reason to yourself about your stupid feelings. Be firm and trust that there is always something better for you, someone else, perhaps, who is your equal in integrity. Forgive and let go of your husband.

You say you love him and so you cannot let go of him? Think about this; imagine him making love with all the women he meets...what do you feel? Be honest with yourself...love yourself first...

The key is "<u>Love yourself first</u> before you can love anyone." You cannot give what you don't have.

12

HARMONY IN MARRIAGE RELATIONSHIP

Marriage relationship is the most critical type of relation, it can make or break a person in his/her life's direction sometimes his whole life through. It is also the most intimate kind of relationship that each of the spouses should have constant and consistent communication with each other to maintain a strong, durable and lasting relationship. There are several stages of the quality of relationship in marriage. The first year is most often more physical attraction and activities between husbands and wives. Then there is the stage where the first child is born followed by some challenges in the marriage such as parenting methods and priorities, financial challenges as the family increases in number when more children come along.

Together both husband and wife learn to face challenges that come along for the sake of their family. They both should have mutual agreement as to how to handle every challenge and issues along the way, challenges about financial condition, household management, parenting, and jobs. To maintain a harmonious relationship in the family, the husband and the wife should have a mutual agreement on every issue in their family. This can only happen when both husband and wife have stable love between them, that kind of love that surpasses any obstacle in life.

Remember that a strong and successful family relationship depends so much on the quality of relationship between the father and the mother. This is the very reason why a single person, man or woman should be discreet and as much as possible avoid nonsense flirtations that may attract the wrong person to become the spouse. One wrong step in this stage of searching for a life partner can ruin a person's life. It is better to start this relationship right and work out and be assertive on it in a moment by moment basis.

There are many ways to be assertive in your relationship with your spouse. Express in your most natural, sincere and loving way what you expect in your marriage and anything that matters to you for both of you.

Below is an example of how I assert my marriage through writing a letter to my husband while we were apart for 5 years. Here's the letter;

To you My Love,

You must have known by now that when I call you "My Love", I really mean it straight from my heart, not just from my head. You know so well that I have had great trouble believing in "Love". I used to be strongly skeptic concerning this matter. My experiences with men, beginning with my Dad cemented in me some notions that men are selfish and self-serving. I just hated men and I thought it stupidity for a woman to love a man...including a husband. But I love you and this changed everything.

I remember those times when I heard my ex-colleagues and friends talking about how much they love their husbands, I would immediately snap out and lashed on them enough to make them feel like they were idiots so that the next time I was around them they saw to it that they must avoid talking about the subjects of love, marriage and sex.

My Dad was an authoritarian religious fanatic. Everything we siblings did in our early childhood must coincide in his strict teachings and dogma. I also discovered that we three siblings were his children with another woman, his ex-student, that Mom is his legal wife but she was barren. This knowledge about our parent's conflicts gave me an idea that a man is self-serving to the point of hurting emotionally even the woman (wife) who is devoted to him. My Mom was a virtuous, loving and devoted wife to my Dad all throughout their whole lives together.

The worse experience I had with a man was my ex-husband. He was the epitome of deceptions, infidelity, womanizing, gambling and of everything that can fill his life with pleasures regardless of whether I am hurt or agree-disagree of what he was doing openly or secretly. For me men are absolute hunters for pleasure and self-gratification and they pursue their desires no matter what the cost. For these types of men, women are basically mere pleasure-object. These men won't care about the real meaning of a happy and fulfilling marriage life. Pleasure is their goddess.

My Love, as you know, you are my third husband and I won't say that it's all my ex-two husbands' fault for the separation or break-up of those marriages. The first was the longest marriage of 18 years. In the first place such marriage was not my idea or preference. I was forced into it and I considered it the greatest disaster that ever happened in my whole life...not only in the way it happened but it turned out as a disaster of having such a vicious husband that confirmed why I hate men. The main reason that it took so long before escaping from that marriage is my wonderful children. My idea was that my children should in their formative years, have a loving father to grow up with...Being a good and loving father to our children was the only credit I can give my first husband.

The second broken marriage was to my second husband and it was nobody's fault for he died after ten years of our marriage. My idea for that marriage was for an escapade...to escape from that hellish first marriage in which my second husband had provided me all the means and opportunity to leave the first. I felt guilty about this marriage because I turned out as a user to the willing participant and most of all was because I didn't really love him romantically, he was just like a father to me. The offer was initiated by him and I saw it as the opportunity for my advantage.

My Love, as you well know by now, I see you as God's gift to me. You are the answer to my lonely prayers and you are the perfect physical manifestation of my heart's desire for a husband. It may be so late when we first had our encounter in the net because I am not young anymore (one of my insecurities) and compared to my first two husbands you are the youngest...what an irony.

But you are My Love...that's what you are ever since the first time I saw you. My feelings for you are confirmed and strengthened when you came to stay with me for almost a month. You may be far physically but I feel like you had always been my husband since time immemorial. Sometimes I would wonder what if you also are the father of my children...everything would have been perfect. I would have the most handsome, beautiful and genius children.

My Love, you are wonderful...the most wonderful man I had ever met and get familiar with. I am sorry for attacking you at times when my mental attitudes about men recur in me. I sometimes bark at the wrong tree which is based on my earlier notions about men. Knowing you and having you as my husband may change my judgment concerning men. In a sense you are actually my hero.

There are just some issues that I would like to clarify which is also the main reason why I am writing this letter to you and for that matter, for the public to read.

1. Building the life you really desire to live.
2. A fulfilling marriage life is equivalent to a generally successful life.
3. Ingredients of a marriage relationship that works.

Building the life, you really desire to live

My Love, I know that between us two, you are the planner and the action person whereas, I am the dreamer and having a clear vision of what I really want in my life. All my life's successes were built in this process and all my life's failures and heartaches were pulled down by my emotion... FEAR.

The deeper I love you, the stronger also the emotion

fear is working to run me down. There are always opposing forces in nature...nature works in opposites in any areas of creation.

The questions I would raise here are the following:

1. What kind of life do you plan to build?

2. Are all your energies focused to pursue and to complete that life?

A fulfilling marriage life is equivalent to a generally successful life.

I had been married twice before we met, the first was 18 years which bore two children and the second was 10 years.

I consider having my wonderful children as one success or dream come true in the first marriage. Educating myself academically and having a good and stable job in the government were another points that I consider as personal success. My ex-husband's delinquent personality had actually turned out as my stepping stone to my personal success. If only he had not let me down I could have gone further to at least becoming a politician in our locality or any other fame in the society...this is inherent in me but my fear of failure due to the unwanted, to say the least, marriage situation I had changed course, my energy was focused on how to leave him and to find another husband who will deserve the honor of having a successful wife.

The success I could consider in my second marriage were the positions I had in the hotel business and my position in the school where I was teaching. It was during this time when I realized that I possessed inherent qualities that could put me on a pedestal; all I needed was a little push from a loved one who truly care for me. There was a conflict though...my children. They didn't like him and the feeling was mutual between them. My son thought he was too old and ugly for me. My daughter feared him because of some cultural influences. With this kind of conflict in the family, my energy goes down and I feel beaten with fears and worries. I did not keep my position up and I was dreaming of a better situation so my focus diverted to focus on the betterment of my children's lives rather than to the marriage. Only when my second husband died did my children's lives became successful.

My Love, I have dream for us both in our marriage and I am opening it here for you to see its viability. I welcome any comment from you.

In my third marriage...this is with you...my focus is in the essence of love. You come to me in perfect timing. My children are now on their own...there will be no conflict, hopefully...It would just be love and loyalty that I need in our marriage and I will be what I really am. My natural me is beauty (attraction), dignity and abundance and I will have all these fueled by your love, our love for each other. Being me, I will always find a niche in any society I am in because I know what I want and I will find it anywhere, anytime; I just have to notice them...your love will show me...in short you are my inspiration.

Ingredients of a marriage relationship that works.

A dynamic marriage relationship leads to success in all areas of life. The question is; what is a dynamic marriage relationship?

First, a dynamic marriage relationship is built in the durable essence of love. Where love is the strong foundation and the instituting power in marriage, nothing can go wrong. Love defies any deficiency, inadequacy, insufficiency and inefficiency, personal, social or general. Love is patient and supportive. Failure has no chance where love is present. Betrayal and deceptions cannot cohabit with love hence they will all scamper away. In a marriage where love dwells abundance in everything also linger on. Abundance in ideas, dreams, material possessions and social position. Love attracts all that is good and pure and repels all that are conspiratorial and deceptive.

A dynamic marriage relationship is one that each partner workout over time to a happy and fulfilling life that they both agree to build.

Conclusion:

My Love, I may sound professorial but I know deep in me that we both know what we want in our marriage and I can see and had witnessed your persistence to have the kind of life that you want to build. Your almost a month stay with me had completely confirmed your love to me and this is all I need in our marriage.

Always remember that I love you and that says it all.

Your wife,
Jenny

13

KEEPING THE LOVE ALIVE IN MARRIAGE

t is common knowledge that many marriage relationships break up. Here in the US divorce is common, in the Philippines there is no divorce but there are many cases of separation. The main reasons of marriage break up is because there is a mutual loss of love between the spouses. There are many ways why love diminish worse is completely gone in the marriage. These are financial reasons lack of it or too much of it that is not managed rightfully. Cheating between spouses is also common.

None of these would happen if there is a soul-deep love in each person. A soul level love retains only the good things both in the person herself and on her spouse.

Love should be the foundation in a marriage relationship, such type of love that can stand through the storm in the marriage.

I am going to elaborate the three types of love that can stand the test of time.

Nothing can compare to the happiness of one who is actually experiencing and enjoying being loved and who can love in the truest sense. Love is a very happy energy that is warming not only the soul but also giving colors to life as a whole. Love begets love; if you love someone unconditionally, you will reap love from him/her/them in multiples. Love is overflowing.

Love is like a seed of any tree or fruit-bearing plants. You plant one seed of love in a very fertile soil and nurture such seed as it grows until it bears fruit; the fruit of such one good seed will yield you thousands even millions of good fruits in its lifetime.

Who do we love? The Bible tells us to love even "your enemies". Well this is tough if we take it literally; we cannot force ourselves to love the "unlovable" and the "misfits" more so the "hateful" enemies. But Love does not qualify, does not "pre-condition" the object of love; and love is freely given without asking for payback. This is the only type of Love that makes us a happy person and which therefore make us enjoy a happy and blessed life in our lifetime.

There are three types if not stages of love. First, we must be a recipient of God's unconditional Love, the Agape Love. To be a recipient of such love is to acknowledge the Existence of God or Nature, praise the Greatness of God or Nature, be awed by the Beauty of Nature or God's Creation. We should take time to be in the "presence" of God or Nature; to be connected and establish a certain degree of strong connection; each of us is also part of nature so we should experience "oneness" to the whole Creation or God, or the Universe; whichever suits your conviction. Only then can we experience this Agape Love; the Unconditional Love that once found a seat within us will have its "throne" to Divinely Guide us as we live our lives. This Divine Guidance functions in every aspect of our lives...it Guides, Protects, Provides, and the list continues.

The second type or stage of love is the Philos; this is the kind of love we accord our relationships with any other human beings in our horizon and the whole population in the world. With this kind of love reigning in our hearts, we can allow everybody to be "them"; we won't "attack" or destroy any one's life in any way, rather we offer encouragement freely when needed. We can only have this kind of love if we experience the Agape Love. People can "fake" Philos love according to their selfish and ulterior motives but the truth will come out sooner than they will realize and it will be shown in the troubled life that they will experience. Learning and surrender to the Source of all Love, the Agape, will then be the only solution. Philos love will be noticeable by people surrounding us, if we have this; we will be popular and be known as an "authentic", reliable, trustworthy, understanding, among others.

In this kind of love also falls the love for parents, children, relatives, associates, best friends, etc.

The third kind or stage of Love is the Eros Love; it is so called because of its natural tendency to be erotic or erroneous, well not literally erotic in the normal sense. This is the love we accord our husband or wife. This is the most sensual and emotional love and can easily be diverted into mere sexual pleasure and lust. This is the most destructive love if not supported by high moral values; hence instead of this love to be a blessing it becomes a curse to humanity and yet people won't realize it. This is the kind of love that blindfolds humanity so that everybody goes down to the pit of destruction. This Eros Love could only be a blessing, a gift of joy and happiness, and be successful if we have Agape Love and Philos Love in the background; other than being backed-up or founded in the Agape and Philos Love, Eros is a tool to destroy humanity in every turn. Just observe what is going on with this kind of relationships these days. Divorce, broken homes, scandals in high places, juvenile criminals as a result of broken homes...look at statistics; the list is endless destruction of human values and lives. And nature is angered resulting to natural disasters and calamities. Can you connect? No, you won't even believe it; but believe it or not. The Bible says "Let those who have eyes see, and those who have ears hear..." Humanity is carnal and spiritually blind; it needs a Love higher than what they are only familiar of.

The Universe Has Provided All the Reasons to be Happy

I had discussed only three basic reasons to be happy in this life but sure I can do much better, given the time and space. This world contains all the reasons to be happy if we see it that way and if we know the Universal Laws the govern it; and most important, knowing is just basic, we should learn to Live What We Know, otherwise head knowledge will just confuse us. The trick is: Live and Experience all you Learn and Know...don't just talk about it.

14

RELATIONSHIP WITH PEER GROUPS

What is a peer group? Peer group relationships start even at an early age. In one way or another each of us stumble into certain groups through the socialization process. Most often, if you are a child of church going parents and family, you instantly belong to a group of other children of the same family membership of a given religious sect. Normally, children are segregated from the adults in church functions during the worship days. In this case a child learns to communicate and relate with other children who they became familiar with in the long run of repeated meetings. Here a child learns to fit himself to the group, he begins to observe and realize whether he is likeable or is rejected by the group because of some reasons. Most common peer groups are blood relatives such as cousins, siblings too especially when the age gaps are close.

This peer group relationship during childhood lays down the foundation of the child's future peer group relationships. When he begins to go to school his classmates become his peer group too and he will start to learn more about his personality in relation to the group. In the class if he excels in the academics his classmates will acknowledge that and this will boost his self-confidence. There are many aspects of personality that can trigger popularity or otherwise that the peer group notice about an individual. Beauty is another notable part of a person that can quickly be recognized but then beauty is not enough to become likeable for peer groups because the peer groups will be part of your functional life in a long term basis so they see not only in the outward attraction but most importantly your inner qualities such as intelligence, kindness or attitudes among others.

What exactly is your inner desire in a peer group? Do you desire to be popular, or just be contented to be a shadow who sits in the corner alone while everybody is partying? Whatever you prefer in a peer group is always right for as long as that is what you want for yourself and that you handle it correctly.

The bottom line is that, being humans, we cannot do away from peer groups relationship, it is a sense of belongingness that keep us going in life.

Human beings are gullible in certain and varied degrees otherwise, one is not human at all or he will be uneducable, worse than being gullible, isn't it?

One significant reason for being gullible is the fact expressed in the statement "No man is an island." People learn from other people in the process of socialization beginning from the smallest unit in society which is the family, peer groups and so on as he continues life's journey. What one becomes is the totality of his socialization processes and his inherent personal qualities. How one perceives and reacts to certain people and relationships, incidents and situation, location and territory, weather or environment, and so forth, comprise the accumulated type of personality one has become.

Reactions to all these life experiences also depend on the inherent mental attitudes and intellectual capacity of an individual. The degree and quality of interactions with all of these life situations also affect the growth and development of a person in every stage. These are just some of the many complexities a human experience and what he becomes; a bully or a gullible?

The treatment one receives and perceives in the family setting at an early stage of development depends a lot on the personality composition of an individual. Some examples are; being the first baby, son or daughter in normally loving parents is favorable to the social standing of such a child; and of course this position has to come with the personal inherent qualities such as beauty or good looks, health and intellectual capacity such as IQ, talents, perceptions, speaking skills, among others.

All these personality components determine the quality of socialization an individual experience in all his developmental stages in life hence also determine his position in the society.

How one becomes a bully or a gullible victim

There are many and varied determinants, like what I had stated above, for one to become a bully.

Given all those favorable and unfavorable socialization processes from the smallest unit of society and, as he lives onwards in the developmental processes, in addition to the inherent gene or nature of the person; a bully must have been into unfavorable, even inhuman treatment in his foundation years, or that he is just a naturally rotten piece of a gene or both.

What is common to both?

Similarly, such conditions apply to a gullible, or the victim of a bully with the apparent reasons that one is a victim and the other the oppressor. Common to both is the unfavorable treatment or a perceived unfavorable as being inculcated to them from the family...unfavorable treatment is broad that includes violence to the extreme and over-protected in the other end; plus the inherent mental attitudes, tendencies, perceptions and other mental capacities in the individual levels.

Like attracts like

Not everybody is a bully nor everybody is a victim of bullies. Given this premise, why would anyone become a victim, to the point of being killed by bullies?

The answer would most probably be "like attracts like" and/or they reciprocate and need one another in order to survive in a world which these two types of personalities perceive as a tough life.

This is something to ponder both for bullies and victims of bullies.

15

RELATIONSHIPS WITH FRIENDS AND BEST FRIENDS

What is the difference between mere friends or acquaintances and best friends?

As social beings and as we continue to develop both physically, emotionally and intellectually, we come across various types of people either casually or unintentionally or for some purposes. Peer groups are more random then it narrows down to a group of friends then to a best friend or best friends.

If you are still working or studying, your colleagues or classmates respectively are your peer groups. In these peer groups you impress certain reputations that can be good or disdainful to the group in general. Such reputations as seeing you as a good cook, as kind, good dancer, having an amazing voice, intelligent, among others are a boost to your self-esteem and self confidence in a peer group setting. The peer group see your personality in a broader sense. Whereas friends see you more in a personal level. Friends know more about your family background and some other backgrounds that are no secrets in your socialization process. Friends believe in your credibility as a person.

A best friend is a special person in your social horizon who is a God-send angel that mirrors your personality. Everything that you are, inside out has something that reflects the personality of your best friend. Your best friend is your sister in the astral level, you cannot pretend to her what you are not because by instinct she knows you, your feelings and your thought processes included. Your best friend becomes so close to you not by accident but it is fate that brings you together in a given time.

There are several stages in our development and along with it is also the development of our personality as knowledge increases. Our friends particularly our best friends also jibe with our personality in a given time and space. There should have been potential best friends as we grow up but we can only acknowledge the real value of friendship after we had been through a lot of situations that require some emotional supports. I remember my first best friend was when I was twelve years old. Many friends and even my parents were surprised why we became best friends, we were complete opposites physically, emotionally and intellectually, but I knew we were best friends because I had this special concerns and feelings for her. When people despised her weaknesses, I took pity on her instead of joining them in their criticisms. I always took side with her in all her flaws. I did not expect anything from her, I just wanted to give and support her. My next best friend was when I was in high school, she was a perfect girl intellectually but she also had flaws which were very acceptable to me. Best friends are human beings too just like you, they have flaws and imperfections, sometimes they are ridiculous but you accept and care for them just because they are your best friends and they are your mirrors in many ways, even in ways that are not obvious.

The bottom-line is to have a real best friend is a blessing in your life because they are your angels and a mirror of your own life whether you are aware of it or not. Just realizing that they are angels in your life in a given time and space is by itself a blessing to you. Remember best friends are soul-level sisters, they are more than blood sisters.

How one perceives and sees himself/herself in the truest sense is also how others would see him/her.

No one can please everybody at all times and in all places; in fact it is easier to be repulsed by everybody than the other way around.

One of the wonders in getting older…hehe; some would say "just getting more matured" is that you become seasoned and you have a lot of things to look back into your earlier existence.

You can look back and see how you handled certain and various situations in all areas of your life. There are a lot to look back and you can see why people at present see you the way they want to see you.

You are what you are as a cumulative result of your personal experiences alongside your individual and personal choices, preferences and your personal reactions to every event of your life in its various phases.

Most people exist by just going along with the flow and God knows where the flow is leading and just react passively on what they encounter along the way.

The following are examples of those I had perceived as my reputation in various stages of my life;

1. At the onset to my awareness of my existence;

    My parents saw me as wonderful and amazing. I had no idea why but that was my feeling, but I also perceived that I was known to be stubborn and having bad tantrum.

2. For my peer group e.g. classmates, friends, cousins and other people surrounding me from my age of puberty and teens years;

    I had perceived that they look up at me as capable of achieving what I wanted and they believed on my ability. I was known to be daring, gutsy and successful in getting what I wanted.

3. In romance I am upright and straightforward. Sweet as sweet can be but also the worst enemy when I perceived that I am being fooled, I am known to "burn bridges" and feel happy about it. I am known to easily replace a stupid lover or a husband if I wanted to; and if I did, friends would applaud me. I am all-heart, service and mind in a romantic relationship but I can instantly shut off my heart if necessary because I believe in "the head is above the heart"…am not a fool in love, I got brains.

4. In my more mature years in school, job and other social groups, I am known to have wide range of knowledge in Humanities and Ethics and Spirituality; frank, straightforward, upright yet not old-fashioned. Some people are scared of me while others love me and idolize me for their own personal

reasons but many dislike me especially the trying hard type of people, the ugly and the born liars.

5. Last but not least, for my family, I am a loving matriarch and for me they are perfect. No one can ever harm my family, no especially my grandchildren. No one can say one bad word or a negative statement to any of my children and grandchildren, I will be the worst enemy for them and I can go down to hell and bring it with me to burn them even in this life. My husband is also my family; never hurt the love of my life.

I know that lots of people would try to be nice to me but they are actually traitors; they betray even themselves. These types of people have no chance to come closer to me because I spew pesticides on them; they are just cockroaches in the dark periphery of life.

The preceding is just among the many techniques on assessing your personal values that become the basis of your reputation to others who know you.

PART II

FEATURED BEST FRIENDS OF MY WHOLE LIFE

1. Ophelia Mulawan
2. Neneng Janulgue
3. Rebecca Beronilla
4. Mina Fernando
5. Violeta Tuto
6. Veronica Malano Miguel

Before I venture on the features of my selected best friends, I would share here the poem I had published in hubpages.com many years ago. It is entitled "Oh Life! Remember, Love, and Faith; the three magic words for Life." The content of this poem reflects the values that I keep dedicated to my loved ones and best friends. Here it goes;

Oh Life! Remember, Love, Faith: the three Magic Words for Life

Life! more than six decades now that we are together;
What have you done to me?
What have I done to you?
What have we done to each other?
Three magic words I learn from you;
Remember; Love; and Faith;
In every stage of our company in this jungle of the living;
These three magic words keep me safe and moving;
When things go wrong, I Remember the happy days with you;
When nothing else could help, I remember to Love you;
When the day is dark and dreary and tomorrow seems bleak, I let Faith guide me and brighten my day and the days ahead of me;
In this lifelong journey I had seen good and bad days;
Met good and bad people and situations;
But the three magic words are my trusted railings as I move higher upward the stairway to my destiny;
Life! I trust in you through the bad and good days;
For I know that you are supportive and reliable;
I value you in every area of this journey;
I count my blessings and discard the useless things along the way;
In this classroom of the living, you are my trusted teacher;
You teach me love, patience, humility, meekness and all the virtues that make all my days colorful and meaningful;
Oh Life! I should know that Life supports itself.

Best friends are angels that life provided us in every step of the way in this life's lifelong journey that we continuously travel on till the Creator claims us to go back to the spirit world when our body become lifeless.

The very reason why I feature my selected and significant best friends here is because they were there in my low times and my best days. They cheer me in my success and they felt sorry for me in my low times. The moments we shared together are most valuable times of my life. They are instruments to mold me the way that I become. They are actually angels to guide me as I walk on in life's journey. They are not necessarily aware of what they had done to my life but I know and I praise and thank God for their presence in my life in any given time.

I remember once when I had no best friend in a certain time when my family had just newly moved to a new place. I had this terrible tantrum feeling so depressed and hopeless for reasons and details I cannot remember now. My daughter who was 14 and in high school who was observing my miserable mood, said to me "Mama why don't you find a best friend, you were never like that when Becky was your best friend, I wish that we still live close to her." This statement of my very own young daughter hit me in the core, that was very true.

So here I will start featuring my best friends beginning my elementary years when I was 12. I will state how we met and how I realized that they are angels to me in a given stage of my development as a human being.

1

OFELIA MULAWAN

It was an innocent friendship to start with. I was a new comeback grade VI pupil in Consolacion Elementary School, a public school in Cagayan De Oro City. I was in that school when I was in grade three but my family moved to the farm in the following year so we siblings had to continue our studies in the public school in that place.

Two and a half years had passed and my Dad said it was time for us to go back to the city; so, in the middle of that school year we siblings had to transfer back to Consolacion Elementary School.

My old classmates when I was in grade three were all in section 1, there were two sections and the classes were homogeneous; those in section 1 were the bright pupils and since I was a transferee, I was put in section 2, the section for dull pupils.

Ofelia approached and happily welcomed me in section 2 class, she introduced herself as the daughter of the barrio captain and that our houses are just separated by a fence; we were actually very close neighbors. Things had changed a lot since we left our house in the city; they were not yet there when we left, somebody else owned that property.

As we started our conversation in school, she asked me why I was in section 2, she said she heard a lot about me and that I was a very bright and honored pupil the last time I was there. I didn't really know why but then it was not a big deal for me, deep inside me knows that I am what I am wherever I am in this planet. As the days went by and as the school year was about to end the school administration and the teachers debated about who should be hailed as the valedictorian. My adviser recommended me but she was opposed with the contention that I was a transferee and that the valedictorian should come from section 1. My advantage at that time was that I was not a mere transferee, I was an old pupil and if I was in section 2 was their mistake. The record showed that I consistently topped on every exams and I was awarded by the Division medals and trophies for making our school the champion in Mathematics, Spelling, Oratorical and other academic interschool contests; I was always the delegate to participate in those contests and I won them all bringing honor to our school. I didn't really care but I noticed that Ofelia was very excited, she was very proud to broadcast that I was her best friend. Yes, we were best friends, we did HomeWorks together in my house and she became very interested in her studies that at the end of the school year I was finally hailed the valedictorian while Ofelia got the third rank in honors.

Sweet memories with Ofelia who idolized me and my self esteem was boosted by having such a best friend. She was very pretty and petite and her family was financially well of; she was very generous to people in need though my family was equally well off too in our neighborhood so, she didn't need to give me any material rewards even after I did everything for her to improve her grades. But she was an angel to me because through our friendship I had learned to acknowledge my personal worth value which I usually took for granted, she was a great inspiration to me. She was the happiest friend I had when I delivered my valedictory address screaming "She is my best friend" although everybody knows that. I really loved her for being what she was in those days.

2

NENENG JANULGUE

She is now Mrs. Trinidad Torres, but I still remember her as Neneng Janulgue.

Like I always reiterate, having a best friend at a certain time of our lives add color and spice to our lives, you can never know what joy they bring into our lives. Best friends are reflections of our personality, they have traits and characteristics that may either be obviously similar to our own or very much opposite. But either way we blend with them in our constant association particularly when the best friends belong to a certain organization.

My best friend Neneng

I never forget Neneng she is a special part of my life though in truth we never had been together for decades now. I used to call her Neneng Janulgue or just Neneng but that was way back in our college days at the Mindanao State University-Iligan Institute of Technology where we were classmates in one of the subjects in our respective courses and we were neighbors too, but now she is officially Mrs. Trinidad Torres. The last time I saw her was I was not yet a grandmother but now I am already a grandmother of eight, eldest of whom is now an Architect, she too is a grandmother now, if not for the media, facebook particularly I would never have known a bit about how her life is going at present. Thanks to facebook.

We were both 24 years old, both married; she had a child while I already had two at that time and life was full of fun and heartaches alternately. We were both struggling to better ourselves and hopefully our lives in the future. We were not sure what life would bring us in our future particularly in our troubled marriage life, we both had some trouble in our love life situations but we had each other to comfort and to show support both moral boost and constant encouragement to each other when times and incidents seemed so difficult.

A best friend in a given time is God's angel sent into our lives to lighten our days and to make life easier to tread on.

Neneng is still my best friend, distance and life changes don't affect on how we regard each other. I always pray for her happiness; she was my angel at the time when I was emotionally unstable; though we just communicate once in a while through the media, she will always be the best friend that I knew.

3

REBECCA BERONILLA

Aside from family and blood relatives best friends are among the most important relationships we can have with other human beings. At the time when we are separated from family or siblings for whatever reasons we find friends in a place where we have no family relations and one or a couple of them would eventually become the best friends. This is a normal tendency for any normal human being.

Most often the best friends that we find in a new place have similar physical, emotional or intellectual capacity with ourselves. They also have similar needs to our own in a given time and space so we can reciprocate with them.

I call her Becky. Becky and I met at the time when I was not sure of my future. I just had developed the attitude "Come what may" to ease my feelings of insecurity and instability in life in general. My two kids were still in elementary and I was worried about their future. My marriage was okay, but okay was not enough because deep in me I had some unanswered questions on why my husband at that time would prefer to be away from home most of the time. I wanted to trust him and in fact finally I was able to eliminate any worries and suspicions about his activities while away from home.

I remember one day during one of my conversations with Becky that I just blurted out to her that my husband had made a woman pregnant in our farm and this statement came out after Becky asked me if my husband would come home on Christmas day.

Becky was an angel in the form of human to help me lighten the burdens that I was carrying in my soul during that time. We can talk about anything that matters in life. We can talk about our children about our income, about our marriage and even about our beauty. Most significant in that friendship at that time was our love life relationship, we had fun in our special ways, we talk about men and to men just for fun, nothing serious because we were both married already.

My friendship with Becky was an unforgettable and important chapter of my life. It was the second longest friendship relationship that I ever have where every day I go to her place from my school before I go home to my children.

Unless you have a best friend like my best friend Becky, you will not know what an angel is that God would send you in your unstable moments in almost every area of your life.

4

BEST FRIENDS, FEATURING MINA MENDOZA AND VIOLETA TUTO

Mrs. Mina Mendoza now but she was single at the time we first met. Simultaneous with our friendship with Mina is Mrs. Violeta Tuto because we three were the new teachers in Suarez High School in 1983.

I will talk first about Mrs. Mina Mendoza, I call her Minahal as an endearment. Minahal and I started our friendship with some undesirable circumstances, I can only smile now whenever I remember it. She is a very strong character just as I am so we clashed in the beginning due to some disagreement but then later on we became the best of friends, we discovered that we can actually agree and reciprocate in many important matters. There are many things I learn from Mina, those things that make me a stronger person in certain areas, her being steadfast and stubborn in a positive way opened my eyes to many truths in life where these values are applicable. One good thing about having a best friend in a certain time of our life is that we can see ourselves in them and we learn a lot about life by just associating with them. We share our values and philosophies in life including some fun. This is the very reason why I value friendship; life is a learning process and best friends are there to learn with. Like I always say, best friends are angels in our lives that God had sent to brighten our days as we travel on in this life.

Mrs. Violeta Tuto who I fondly call Violy is another sweet angel in my life. Mina was hired in Suarez High School in June of 1987 followed by Violy in July and I was hired in August of the same year. We came to the school one month after the other. Best friends have various character traits and backgrounds. What I like most about Violy is she is the type of person who is very sincere in all her dealings to the point that I can see her as having a childish viewpoint about life. She has pure innocence and sincerity that amazed me lots of times. She is meek and could easily forgive those who deliberately demean her; such wonderful and rare human characteristic. We were much younger when we were together, I don't know how she is now; it's been decades that we have not seen each other.

The most important reason why I value friendship and my best friends is that they inculcated important value systems in me in their own unique and special ways. They are truly my angels in a given time and space.

5

BEST FRIENDS FEATURING ENGINEER VERONICA MALANO MIGUEL

The importance of having good and harmonious relationships with best friends in various stages of one's life cannot be bargained.

I had discussed here previously about some of my past best friends. The idea is not to compare them from one another but to show how and why I consider all my best friends in various stages of my life as God-sends, they are like angels in human forms who opened my mind in many situations in their unique special ways respectively. By just being around them lightens my spirit in a manner that only a best friend's presence can fill.

My best friend Engineer Veronica Malano Miguel (Ma'am Veron):

If I have one word to describe Ma'am Veron it's the word "honesty" then if I may add another word to emphasize it, it would be 'sincerity" then collect all the clans of these words such as integrity, credibility, dependability, genuine and so on and on.

Ma'am Veron is very beautiful to me because I only see the beauty of her soul that is reflected in her outward and physical appearance.

In the very long years (three decades approximately) that we had been in close contact with each other my life had started to shape into what I am now; she is a very positive influence and an inspiration that even when we are now apart physically, I am still tickled and would literally laugh when I remember those things we used to do especially in the area of raising our spiritual maturity. Ma'am Veron is an angel not only to me personally but also to my family. She was there in my ups and downs of my life and my family's life; I knew that there were times that she was annoyed by my seeming carelessness like she thought I didn't care what was going to happen in my life and in my future and in this case she would raise a question such as "What is your important variable n life?" She had no idea that questions as such literally lingers on in my mind until I was finally enlightened.

Three decades as being best friends gradually changed our attitudes and outlooks in life hence also guided us to the attainment of what we really wanted to achieve in each of our lives. Although we were going in opposite directions in our life's destiny, we are still successful in each of our life's choices.

This is one most significant reason, among others, why I emphasize best friends in my discussions in relationships.

Printed in the United States
By Bookmasters